THE FIELD

THE FIELD

MARTIN GLAZ SERUP

LES FIGUES PRESS

THE FIELD

[c]: Martin Glaz Serup
&: Les Figues Press
[2011]

COVER: Lise Harlev
TEXT DESIGN: Mathias Kokholm
Translated from the Danish by Christopher Sand-Iversen
ISBN: 978-1-934254-23-3
Library of Congress Control Number: 2011930887

THANKS: Coco Owen, Luke Quattrocchi & Chris Hershey-Van Horn

The Field has been published in Denmark as *Marken* by Edition After Hand and in Finland as *Kenttä* by Savukeidas Kustannus in translation by Esa Mäkijärvi. *The Field* is also available on UbuWeb.

kornkammer [mgs]: www.kornkammer.blogspot.com
les figues press: www.lesfigues.com
ubuweb: www.ubu.com

ƒ

LES FIGUES PRESS
Post Office Box 7736
Los Angeles, CA 90007
USA

This is a nature poem which is also concerned with other things, other things do exist. Three cold greenhouses, their damp industry, yellow in the mist in the field, can you feel like the field, how can you identify yourself with it, with such a place, with a ploughed field, a strange open space, a body without organs.

The field ought to take more exercise, it knows it only too well, it doesn't go to a fitness centre, it takes the car to work. The field doesn't know when it would find time to exercise, the field doesn't understand how everybody else finds time to exercise, what they give up. The field gave up smoking a long time ago, but not smoking isn't enough.

On a trip to Paris without the kids the field asks, do you think we're having a crisis. Yes, comes the immediate reply. A little too immediate, the field feels, it hadn't expected that, the field falls silent. It has to spend a little time working out what needs to be said.

The field spends far too much time on Facebook.

The field spends far too much time watching TV.

The field spends far too little time exercising.

According to the field's nearest and dearest the field spends far too much time on the toilet in the mornings. The field just sits there, waking up. The field is a slow waker.

The field sometimes thinks it's unhappy in a mild and ordinary way that makes it happy because it thinks that it's probably perfectly normal, and that makes it happy because it thinks things could be much worse, which makes it afraid because it thinks things could still get much worse, so it tries to think of something else.

The field has never been outside Europe.

The field has difficulty being where it is, it sounds like a cliché, but that's how it is. The field texts a lot, the field surfs the net a lot, the field is afraid of missing out on something, the field is on-the-go. It keeps itself up-to-date, it wants to know what everybody else is doing right now.

The field isn't particularly interested in nature, nature lover isn't
a word you'd think of when you think about the field, it's not
interested in animals or trees or flowers or whatever it is about
nature that nature lovers are interested in. The best experience
of nature the field has had was at the fair ground in Roskilde; it
went up in a little aeroplane, there were four people in the plane,
it was very intimate, nature is beautiful seen from above, the
plane was red.

The field used to love dancing, drinking and dancing, but after someone took pictures with a mobile phone at a company party and passed them round, it hasn't quite been the same. The field has noticed it's become more inhibited.

Sometimes the field thinks about whether the sea is blue because the sky is blue, that's what it's heard, that the sea reflects the sky, but then how can it be, it thinks, that the water in indoor swimming pools is blue too, what's it reflecting, it can't work it out. Maybe it's because of the blue tiles in the pool, that's what some say, but then again, that doesn't explain why the water in the sea is blue. No. The field lets it lie.

Speaking of the relation of sea to sky, the field thinks, there are more similarities than just the colour. Both are, in one way or another, in opposition to the town. Both are open spaces without many buildings, yet both are controlled by a mass of invisible paths and roads and regulations. There are frontiers between different countries in the air and sea, the field finds this paradoxical, that there are frontiers between countries, there are fixed routes for ships and planes, motorways and side streets and country roads, the field gives no further thought to country roads, the fun stops there. Both the sea and the sky are constantly being monitored and mapped, again and again and again, by meteorological institutes and intelligence services. The weather, the field knows, is the most watched TV programme in the world.

The field can't imagine anything outside of capitalism, the field can't imagine capitalism. Or socialism. Or a third way. Or a fourth. The field isn't exactly sure what it is expected to imagine, or on the whole, what is expected.

If the field were to take an interest in an animal, a species of animal, if it somehow was forced to, had to choose, it would probably be the bird.

The field thinks about exile, how some people become exiles without moving, without migrating, by refusing to leave the place where they were born, the place where they grew up, and which they only leave in order to die.

The field thinks that the fear of being cheated is the most unappealing.

The field thinks that stinginess is an unappealing quality and that it, in some way or another, is related to the fear of being cheated.

The field thinks it has observed a kind of poetic justice in practice in the sense that it is often those who are most afraid of being cheated who most often do get cheated. In the same way that more than half of all people who have been subjected to an unmotivated violent assault will be subjected to one again. Thinking about this makes the field anxious.

The field tries to ignore it when people take pictures of it. Mainly, perhaps, because it feels embarrassed, more embarrassed on the photographer's behalf than particularly self-conscious. Embarrassed about what it sees as the photographer's exaltation at conquering the motif. The field thinks, can't those photographers even experience anything without seeing it through a lens first, and the field feels ashamed at what it sees as the banality of its own thoughts, the cultural conservatism, whatever that means. Cultural conservatism is no positive term in the field's book.

It's funny, the field thinks, by which it means something like strange, that repetition in itself results in a kind of pleasure, that it's a pleasure to revisit somewhere you've been before just because you've been there before, that the same smell or taste, the same sight, the second time, before trivialisation, is a pleasure.

The field finds it almost blasphemous that you can get used to
the beauty of nature, that you can take it for granted, that you can
stop noticing it. That you suddenly just cross the beach as if you
had to get somewhere, that you no longer stop to appreciate the
view, the white mountain tops on the horizon, the stormy sea. That
you no longer see the deep red colour of the clouds at sunset,
that you just think, well it must be getting on toward evening
now, or, well that was that day, or whatever it is you think around
that time. The field has made a rule; every day it must spend at
least two minutes looking at something beautiful in nature for
the sake of beauty alone. The field times it on its mobile. The
leaves, the birds, the beefy, colourful toadstools on the forest
floor. It feels a bit stupid standing there staring like that. No longer
remembers what the point of it all was; a leaf, a bird, a toadstool
and so on, and each of them is indeed pretty, but, the field feels
like shouting, so what. Isn't everything pretty in a way, if you just
look at it for long enough. It's afraid someone will come and find
it looking, will wonder what's going on, will ask if it's okay, will ask
what it's doing. It doesn't know.

The field feels ashamed of taking pictures.

The field tries to pretend nothing's happening.

Once while drunk on holiday in Tenerife, the field tried to explain
its feelings about photography to some random strangers in a bar.
What exactly it was that was shameful about taking pictures. The
field had to resort to a picture: the field felt ashamed of taking
its camera out of its pocket in front of a potential motif, like the
hunter who, next to the nature lover, sheepishly gets his gun out
and in an effort not to attract too much attention shoots one of
the animals being admired. The field got carried away with the
scenario, weren't there also certain affinities between the camera's
flash and the flash from the barrel of the gun. The strangers
couldn't see it. Perhaps they didn't catch it all. The field's English
isn't the best.

The field wants to change its life.

The field doesn't believe in shock treatments or hey presto solutions, the field believes in fundamentally changing its life, the field frequently tries to change its life.

The field sometimes speculates about the specifically masculine and the specifically feminine, whether they exist, it thinks they probably do, but what does this specificity consist of. It doesn't know. It has to give up one careful attempt to find out after another. All the same, it feels sure that a certain essentialism exists, that gender is in itself accompanied by difference. But how. The field doesn't get any further, the field tires of such thoughts, it feels uninspired and wonders whether it can manage a turn on its bike before lunch.

The field is a lot.

The field goes on a trip to London to see one of the statues from Easter Island in the British Museum with its own eyes. It's cheaper to go to London than to Easter Island. When it comes down to it, it doesn't like it anyway, it refuses to ask for help, it refuses to ask if anyone would be so kind as to take that picture. It eats baked beans with Tabasco sauce on toast and eggs at the hotel in the morning and goes home again.

The field isn't interested in pesticides.

The field thinks it makes no difference what it's interested in, the field will in any case have forced upon it and be exposed to both this and that, no matter what it's interested in, and that's what you have to take notice of, in the field's opinion.

The field loves talking on the phone, the intimacy of it, being
together without being together, the sound of the other person in
that person's own sitting room, the sudden nearness that can be
broken off as you wish like turning off the TV. It can talk for several
hours until its ear gets warm and dark red and throbbing.

When the field was a child *The sun is so red, mother* was always sung at bedtime. It was one of the nice Danish folk songs, the field always thought, very comforting, it smelled of mother. The field doesn't feel like this any more, things are different now. The field saw a man on television explain why this song was so sinister, why you should never sing this song to your children, how it was about death, why you shouldn't sing about death to your children. This song, the man said, this song is too harsh, this song is like a threat, this song turns children into frightened and dependent individuals; *the sun is so red, mother/and the woods grow so black*, the man said, indicates the autumn of life, the last moment before the spark of life is extinguished, before it's all over. *Now the sun is dead, mother/and day has passed away*, the man said, *The fox is passing by outside, mother/we must lock our hall*, the man said, is about death passing by outside. The fox is metonymically related to the sun through the colour red, and the sun is dead. The fox is metonymically related to passing away because it is passing by outside, and he who passes away dies. The fox is a predator, the man said, it lies in wait, the man said, and the little singing boy knows it, the man said, he naïvely thinks he can lock death outside by locking the door, but it's not the same thing, you can't, the man said, and he knows it. *Come and sit by my side, mother/and sing a little song*, the man said, establishes that the little singing boy is lying down, as in a coffin, as in a grave, in his bed, horizontally with his last wish, a little song, before he closes his eyes forever,

before he slips into the big sleep, just a song, and he is granted it,
said the man, a song with this rhythmical mother mother mother,
mor mor mor, like a recurring blow, 'mor' as in death or 'mor'
as in Mord or 'mor' as in mort, the man said, and you shouldn't,
therefore, sing this song to your children at bedtime, the man said,
subconsciously they understand that you wish them dead, that you
wish they wouldn't wake up again, subconsciously these children
will feel guilt at having survived, at having in this way disappointed
their parents, because of this song. Do you really think so, asked
the journalist on TV. Yes, the man said, I'm certain.

The field likes to drink hot drinks in the summer, cold ones in the winter.

The field thinks of itself as a very sensitive soul, that it notices small, fine details, colours and smells and moods, and with a certain amount of pride, thinks that this is typical of it.

The field suffers from fear of lifts.

The field is, after having seen *The Birds* as a child, not comfortable around birds.

The field is a very sensitive soul.

The field likes pretty hands.

The field is fond of long legs.

Tits or arse, the field is a tit-field.

The field looks mainly at the eyes, at the look in them.

The field notices shoulder blades.

Stepfamilies, what to think of them, the field doesn't have any particular opinion, it has merely noted that they are the norm now, the normal, that the phenomenon no longer warrants any special attention, whether it's good for the children, whether it's bad. Is it possible to imagine that it could even be skill-developing for the children, like a kind of long group examination, yes, the field thinks, yes, it's not entirely impossible, but if you inquire more closely, it doesn't feel like explaining or developing the thought further.

The field thinks of the word proprietary; it doesn't know what it means.

The field enjoys looking at snow-covered fields.

The field doesn't know what to think about the risk of brain
tumours caused by radiation from mobile phones. The field
has thought about it, it doesn't have an opinion. It's so easy to
always have an opinion about this and that, the experts express
opinions for and against with equal conviction, with equally
strong arguments, it would seem, which almost reduce the risk
of brain tumours caused by radiation from mobile phones to a
matter of personal taste. The field doesn't have an opinion. Is it
so pressing, the risk of brain tumours caused by radiation from
mobile phones, the objective analysis is to a greater and greater
degree dependent upon the viewer's, listener's, reader's personal
sympathies and antipathies towards the various experts and
parties in the dispute. It's entertainment, you have to take it as
entertainment, according to parameters that relate to whether it's
interesting, if anything's happening, if it's surprising, whether you
can be bothered to watch it again and again, whether, as with the
weather, you can be bothered to keep yourself up to date. The
field has yet to decide whether it can be bothered to keep itself
up to date with the risk of brain tumours caused by radiation from
mobile phones.

When the field was little, its greatest desire was to own a penny-farthing.

The field isn't sure if it's too self-obsessed, but it's been feeling better about itself since it started cycling to work.

The field doesn't like electric light, it feels that it is somehow false. The field doesn't like the sound of lawnmowers, but it likes the smell of freshly mowed grass.

We raked the field lightly, it's the old custom, the birds and the poor must also be replete. The field thinks of the Danish folk song, that it's a terribly naïve view of life, about all those resources that might in this way have gone to waste, about when the poor could have known that it was okay to sneak out into the field, stealing, and when it would be a serious theft. An inscrutable system, irresponsible, if the poor are to be fed it must for the sake of everybody's dignity, they should be fed in the workhouse, in the church, in an organised framework, organised by people who take care of things like that. And the birds, a feeder. The field wonders whether it was really like that, in reality, whether it can be true, if the good peasant really raked his field lightly out of a vague feeling of custom and some unclear idea or another of everything's possible interrelation. Out of fear of disapproving glances from the other peasants. Or whether it isn't quite simply the poet's fantasy, the field thinks so, something that sounds nice in songs for dances and on Sundays, nothing that really is about anything, which is to say a work of poetry, just as long as you remember this, that it's a poem, that it's embellishment, just as long as you keep that in mind, then it's a lovely song.

The field isn't sure if it's too self-obsessed, but it's been feeling better about itself since it started going to yoga.

When the field puts its ear to the ground it can hear a faint
humming.

The field has been feeling better about itself since it started going to violin classes once a week; it has dropped out of the Spanish course, which took up a lot of time and they didn't learn enough.

The field likes delightful baroque oboe music.

The field doesn't understand people who are obsessed by teletext.

The field is puzzled by the fact that various cultural personalities from time to time expatiate any and everywhere about politics. Always critically. Often it's something to do with defence or foreigners or the schooling system, the markets are always a kind of villain, nothing's ever good enough. Suddenly you're some kind of Nazi if you vote for one of the conservative parties. The field is puzzled by the view of life this expresses and by this analysis or whatever it is, a kind of hate perhaps, that peeps out, a prejudice: that the whole world lives as if this were the last day, that for many it's merely a case of earning money and spending as much of it as possible before the shops close and that this in itself should be a bad thing. The field doesn't understand this criticism. The field finds it naïve and strange and wonders where it actually comes from. It's a mystery. The field is convinced that many who voice this criticism, that many who directly or indirectly accuse working people with conservative values of being complacent, superficial consumer fetishists, are, perhaps without even having realised it themselves, hypocrites. That they in reality also support various restrictions and other limitations that ensure the country's high standard of living in comparison to most other countries, even though they, when the opportunity arises, in public, at dinner parties, when the opportunity arises, demonstratively distance themselves from the opinions and the very policies that make it possible for many of them to even attend these dinner parties, which swim in red wine and put their opinions about. It is these opinions and this very politics that make it possible for them to even make their opinions heard in the public sphere. Democracy, Arts Funding, Freedom of Speech. Don't they even understand these things, the field thinks. The field basically finds many of these opinion-mongers sympathetic but also, as stated, naïve. Dreamers. The field thinks to itself that many of these opinion-mongers have never really grown up, that they, to put it bluntly, haven't understood the seriousness of it, that they, under cover of being idealists, behave quite irresponsibly, not just in relation to the markets, the environment, the nation, and the individual, but also in relation to their own children, to whom they owe the future.

On a holiday at a manor house, a romantic weekend without the
kids, info material about the place, its history and, in particular,
the surrounding pastures, lies on the pillows. Personally, the field
would probably have preferred chocolate. There is a harvest twice
a year, transgenic rasp germinates after ten years, the air quality
is measured on a weekly basis, the risk of running animals over is
highest at the edge of the woods, the field reads on; here at the
castle lived a woman who according to legend cut off the fingers
of peasant children who stole ears of corn. The field puts the
info material away and asks if they shouldn't do something fun.
They could go for a walk and maybe see a little egret. No. The
little egret is not that probable. The field can't sleep at night, are
you asleep, the field whispers, there is total silence but for deep
breathing and the sound of the cross-country fully automatic
robotic combine harvesters that work around the clock. The field
can't fall asleep. The field lies there thinking; no, the field thinks,
no, the sound of cross-country fully automatic robotic combine
harvesters isn't a romantic sound.

The field considers the relation between sound and silence, whether there is a relation, from what perspective one ought to consider such a relation. Again it probably depends on where you want to go with it, the field thinks. The field considers the relation between sound and silence and loneliness. Sometimes it doesn't feel lonely until it puts some music on, sometimes not until the moment it stops. The relation between music and not-music, then. Even though: the sound of birds, the sound of rain, the sound of neighbours, the sound of a TV in an empty room, the sound of the wind blowing something or other about, all this can have more or less the same effect on the field, as something that starts something and stops something else, as something that in its presence, its appearance, or its absence reveals or conceals, but not in a simple taxonomy—no, the field thinks and lets the thought go, no, it's not as simple as all that.

Essentially, the field doesn't believe that ugliness exists, beauty is easy to imagine, but ugliness.

The field thinks that hearing as a sense will make a comeback in the near future.

When the field passively consumes extreme pictures and stories, typically about war, child abuse, pornography, it wonders what they do to it. It thinks that these stories and pictures are now in it, that they are now a part of the field, of its experiences and life. Perhaps it makes no difference what you consume, but isn't valorisation of an active formation of experience above a passive one both problematic and one-eyed. The field can't make up its mind.

To feel at home, what's that, apart from, of course, important. The field can't imagine that you can actually feel at home in the city's public housing, that anybody does. The field can't imagine anything other than that everybody who lives in such a place thinks only of getting away. That they want to own a house, a garden, that that's all they dream of.

They talk of where to go on holiday. The field finds it magical that Tycho Brahe lies buried under a red gravestone in the church with the two towers on the main square in Prague. Just think, thinks the field, he ate himself to death and had a nose made of silver. The field would like to visit Prague.

The field has had almost no days off work in its life, the field is a strong field, it's in good health, in good spirits. That's what the field thinks of itself, that it's solid, a solid field, one you can count on.

The field has been a field as far back as it can remember, the field
is a field in all weathers.

The field has been well-dressed most of its life, the field is still well-dressed, always dressed in something fitting, something neutral, something considered, something ordinary, but always with that little thing, that something extra, a fun detail, something loud or something handed-down or something else.

The field sees an interview on TV with a musician who says of himself that what he says has never made any impression on him, he's never taken himself very seriously, and in fact he still doesn't. This makes a great impression on the field, who doesn't understand one iota of what it means, for the musician must know what he means and says and say what he means and so on, but it makes a great impression on the field all the same. The field has never heard anything of the sort. That it's possible to talk like that, think like that. The interviewer doesn't understand either, what do you mean, he asks the musician, the musician answers: no fear, no envy, no evil. This reassures the field somewhat, it sounds like an artist's slogan, so the musician is a typical artist: no doubt good at his thing, but detached from reality and non-committal. The field doesn't need to consider what he says that much and perhaps that's what the musician means, the field thinks, that you shouldn't take any notice of it, that it's just for fun.

The field has thought about it, it has reached the conclusion that it's better to not understand something than to misunderstand it. The field has thought about it, it has reached the conclusion that the most interesting things in reality don't happen in reality but in people's heads, in the imagination.

The field thinks about the poplars it sees, along the side of the road, two by two, like a sort of people, quite still, that it's a fitting name for such a plant: poplar as in popular.

The field thinks it French kisses too little, that there is far too long between outbursts of spontaneous passion.

Actually the field has never really liked French kissing, it finds it, in some way or another, camel-like. It likes the idea of spontaneous passion, even though, when it comes down to it, dates aren't the worst thing in the world, something you can look forward to, prepare for, a place where you know what's going to happen when, where there's time, where there's space.

The field thinks there's too little time, too little space, too little sex in its life.

You can do anything, walk in anywhere, open a door, stop people
on the street, kiss them, hit them, you can smash a window, jump
out somewhere, overturn something, steal a car, sweep someone's
courtyard, feed the animals, shoot them, you can strip anywhere,
turn out the light, hang up, say anything you like to anyone you
like, interrupt, sing, what's the worst that can happen, what's the
worst that can happen: thinking about it makes the field feel
insecure.

The field remembers when it was younger, they did it all over
the place, it was difficult to relax while doing it, the field was
constantly afraid that someone would come and who it might be
and what they might say.

The field finds words such as euphemism challenging.

The field remembers when it was younger; when it realised how a kaleidoscope works, mirrors, not magic, the disappointment, that feeling, like being abandoned by oneself, like having one little part of the world exchanged for another, coarser. The experience was a little brutalisation, the field thinks, but then again that's probably too much said, that's probably making too much of it. There are pictures of the field from when it was younger; pictures of the field when it was little, pictures of the field a little older, pictures of the field grown up, as a child, as a youth, older. The field in sun, the field in snow, the field alone and with others, the field in the field with the Boy Scouts by a bonfire. There isn't a district of the field's life, no single region, no time, that isn't thoroughly documented. The photographs are kept in big boxes in the attic, the field never looks at them.

Cat owners and dog owners, the field considers what you say about them, about the differences between them. Whether you can extrapolate something fundamental about people's characters by observing which animals they surround themsevles with. Maybe there's something in it, the field thinks, it's in any case true that cat owners are lazy individuals who don't take responsibility and don't want to be dependent on anything, but it could all the same be nice, so cosy, the field thinks, with a little ball of fur that takes care of itself and shits outside. Cat owners are half-hearted and tough people. The field hates dogs.

The field is peculiarly touched by teddy bears on children's
clothes, it's really quite odd, the field thinks, that this should touch
it, since the field really doesn't like teddy bears.

The field speculates about what it means to be touched by something. For the field, being touched is like a hand that closes carefully around something warm and water balloon-like in its insides, for example when it sees teddy bears on children's clothes. It really doesn't like it.

The field really doesn't like liver, no matter where it comes from, whether raw or grilled.

The field really doesn't like oilcloths, but it can see that they're practical.

The field likes caves and mussel shells; the field likes secretive things in general.

Isn't it more and more the case that there is an incredible amount of meaningless communication—the field thinks there is, the field thinks that all this communication takes up too much space, all these social networks, all these text messages, all these sounds, this blinking, whirring, humming, and bleeping, what's the point of it the field thinks and fears it has become reactionary, has grown too old too soon, what's the point of it, if you didn't know better, it thinks, you'd think that all this wireless-hypermobile-eternally-present and always online technology's primary aim was to keep the users or consumers occupied and on-the-go, occupied with communicating, communicating, in order to, in this way, keep the consumers away from other areas, for example consideration of their habits and needs.

The view doesn't interest the field, it doesn't have a calming effect on it, it had heard it's supposed to be something special. The field tries to feel it, the wide open spaces, the clear sky. No. It's not for it. No. All that space, it doesn't seep into the field as a calm, the open landscape, it's something you hear others talking about. The field thinks it overrated. Eccentric. To have space, but if the space is just empty, what's it for. The field is sure there's something it hasn't understood, everyone else has understood it, there's a code it hasn't cracked yet. It looks; but what is it supposed to see, there isn't anything.

But the landscape, the field can be jealous of the landscape
from time to time, the landscape doesn't have any colleagues it
has to see again and again, the landscape doesn't have friendly,
superficial conversations in the kitchenette with them; the
landscape, the field thinks, doesn't find itself at a Christmas lunch
confessing all to a boss. The field considers phoning in sick but
gets on its way all the same, luckily it's only at work until 3 o'clock.
But the landscape, what was it about the landscape, the field
has the feeling it had an important thought in connection with
the landscape that has stayed with it, the memory of a thought
it had, oh yes, the field hits on it again; the landscape has a
very democratic structure, that was what it thought, because
there is at first sight nothing in the landscape that is objectively
more important than anything else, all elements are equal in a
landscape—but are they now, the field isn't sure, aren't the large
things, the sea, the hill, the sun, the forest, for example, not
privileged in relation to the smaller things, the reeds, the rushes,
the sand, the stones, no, no, actually the field doesn't think they
are, the sand that makes up the beach, each individual tree in
the forest, the birds in the flock—and alone—they are just as
important, just as beautiful, the rustling of the leaves, but then the
field isn't sure again, isn't sure whether you can call it democratic,
for isn't democracy a form of government, a form in which
everybody has, in theory, just as much say, and even though the

hill and the sun aren't more important than the leaf and the stone, there isn't really anyone who governs a landscape, a landscape is probably precisely the most directionless thing you can imagine, the field thinks, a landscape isn't underway, a landscape doesn't experience populist coup attempts—and yet: no, the field doesn't know enough about biology, enough about flora and fauna or whatever it's called, it doesn't know enough about cultivation and production to dare follow that trail; in any case, glaciers and wandering dunes exist and you speak of the migration of trees and the earth's crust that moves just so many centimetres a year—how to understand it in the light of democracy—the field doesn't know. The field would like to talk to someone about it, but whom. And how would you actually start such a conversation, the field doesn't know. The field wishes its brooding would soon be disturbed, that the telephone would ring, that the smoke alarm would start wailing. It doesn't.

The feeling of claustrophobia is very real. The field frequently feels this way; as if it really were in a very small room. The problem with the feeling of claustrophobia is that you can't leave it behind, the problem with the feeling of claustrophobia is that it follows you. Maybe it isn't a feeling of claustrophobia, the field thinks, maybe this is just how it feels to be unfit.

Time travel, the field has no opinion about it. It is a natural part of children's books and science fiction films, but apart from that, nah. In any case, it's as though everybody from all ages is already here at the same time and sometimes, the field thinks and is slightly amused, it feels like sending some of them back to where they came from. Or on. But what would be the good of it, the field thinks, that place doesn't exist, backwards, forwards, the situation is the same, they are all always present with their strange clothes and their opinions and their smells, their insights, plans of action, emotional life, their collective values. What would be the good of moving any of it around. Like deciding, with immediate effect, to stop peeing at one end of the swimming pool. Time travel, no. The field can't see the point of it. All you get out of occupying yourself with time travel is a lot of bother. It's difficult to get ahold of fuel for such journeys and it is always impressed upon the travellers that they are absolutely not allowed to touch anything, that it could have unforeseeable consequences for the present— and so what, the field thinks. The field doesn't understand the apparently uncritical and eternal celebration of the status quo. Everything we touch in the present already has unforeseeable consequences for the future, but that doesn't cause anybody to suggest we stop. Or almost nobody. No. Time travel. No. The field can't be bothered to concern itself with it.

The field can't, it's tried all morning, think of the word improper. Independent, irresponsible, unfeeling, no, exposed, no, it can't think of it. When it manages to later in the day, finally, the field speculates about whether it's important that it's precisely this word its subconscious represses, it speculates about whether it perhaps should seek professional help. The field thinks about what otherwise might lie hidden, which words and which reasons for forgetting them, whether it might be serious, whether it might be something it wants to be confronted with. The field realises it's wringing its hands and stops immediately.

ACKNOWLEDGEMENTS

Excerpts of *The Field* have appeared or will appear in the following magazines: *La Otra* and *Levrel* (Mexico); *Spring* and *Den Blå Port* (Denmark); *Tuli&Savu* (Finland); *PRECIPICE* (Canada); and *OEI* (Sweden). The author is grateful to Víctor Rodríguez Núñez, Denis Gómez García, Katherine M. Hedeen, Marianna Kurtto and Christopher Sand-Iversen for the translations.

The Field has been sculpturly installed at Kunstnersammenslutning Jylland's exhibition in Århus Kunstbygning 2008 (Denmark) and as part of NOT CONTENT, curated by Les Figues Press at Los Angeles Contemporary Exhibitions 2010 (USA). http://www.notcontent.lesfigues.com.

Martin Glaz Serup would like to thank The Danish Arts Council, The Danish-German Writer's Retreat at Hald Hovedgaard [April 2009], Teresa Carmody, Vanessa Place and Gitte Broeng.

Martin Glaz Serup was born in 1978 and has published three chapbook-essays, six collections of poetry, and six children's books, most recently an illustrated story entitled *When granddad was a postman* (2010). Serup is the former founding editor of the Nordic web-magazine for literary critism *Litlive* and the literary journal *Apparatur* and managing editor of the poetry magazine *Hvedekorn*. He has been teaching creative writing at The University of Southern Denmark and at the writer's school for children's literature at The University of Aarhus and is now working as a ph.d. student at the University of Copenhagen. In 2006 Serup received the Michael Strunge Prize for poetry and in 2008 he received a Gold medal from The University of Copenhagen for his dissertation on poetry and relational aesthetics. He is blogging at www.kornkammer.blogspot.com.

Christopher Sand-Iversen was born in Cardiff, United Kingdom in 1981. He studied art history at the Courtauld Institute of Art in London and photography at Fatamorgana, the Danish School of Art Photography. He is currently a M.A. candidate in the Visual Culture program at the University of Copenhagen and runs a small art gallery in Copenhagen. He has translated a number of books from Danish into English.

LES FIGUES PRESS
Post Office Box 7736
Los Angeles, CA 90007
USA